PAUSE+PRAY

pause+pray.

franciscan
media®
Cincinnati, Ohio

ISBN 978-1-63253-451-4

Published by Franciscan Media
28 W. Liberty St.
Cincinnati, OH 45202
www.FranciscanMedia.org

Printed in the United States of America.

Contents

Introduction

A friar-colleague once posited that St. Francis, "was a blank screen on which we project our own impressions." Fair enough— so here's my projection. Though Francis of Assisi is celebrated for his love of the natural world, I feel that he could also be known as the patron saint of humble prayer.

Francis understood the spiritual and psychological toll that modern life could bring. His tired feet carried him to faraway lands to spread the Gospel, and yet he craved solitude so acutely he would hide out in caves to recharge. Understandable given the task laid before him: He was a repository of the good news and a channel by which that news spread to the world. Little wonder he craved solitude!

But none of his life's work would have been possible without a vibrant and complex prayer life. Though medieval to his core, Francis struggled with social ills not uncommon today: political infighting, civil unrest, even disease that lurked along the periphery. He struggled as his order grew, carrying the weight of his calling even when his body began to fail him. How did he cope with these burdens? How did he recenter?

By all accounts, he prayed. Through prayer, he celebrated the world around him: (*"All praise be yours, my Lord, through all that you have made."*) It is where he longed for peace: (*"Happy those who endure in peace, by you, Most High, they will be crowned."*) And it was how he embraced his own mortality: (*"All praise be yours, my Lord, through Sister Death, from whose embrace no mortal can escape."*) Prayer was both Francis's compass and his destination: his every step and his journey's end.

We at Franciscan Media understand the importance of prayer and how difficult it can be to fit it into a day. Thus, we created a free resource to remedy that, a daily email called *Pause+Pray* (FranciscanMedia.org/pausepray), offering gentle coaching each morning to start the day prayerfully. It was so popular that it was adapted into the book you are reading right now.

We think Francis of Assisi would be proud. Because prayer, to him, wasn't simply communion with the divine. It was his sacred call to action. And that's how each prayer is structured in these pages. We encourage you to pause—to quiet the noise in and around you. Then you are guided to reflect on a theme, pray on it, and perhaps greet the world with different eyes.

I like to think that Francis, in the recesses of a cave or a hermitage somewhere in central Italy, felt a kind of reset after prayer. It obviously fueled his leadership of the order. "The friars...should work in a spirit of faith and devotion and avoid idleness," he wrote, "which is the enemy of the soul, without however extinguishing the spirit of prayer and devotion, to which every temporal consideration must be subordinate."

This book is a humble continuation of that directive. Family, career ambition, the search for joy or wellness or meaning—all noble pursuits. But unless they are built on a foundation of prayer, how strong is that foundation? Prayer fortifies. It clarifies. It gives us direction and the permission to start over. So, in the spirit of Francis of Assisi, let us begin again....

Christopher Heffron
Editorial Director | Franciscan Media

gratitude.

The Great Thanksgiving

Bruce Epperly

reflect

A meaningful life begins with gratitude, the great thanksgiving for the whole of your life and all creation. It is giving thanks for everyone who has made—and continues to make—a difference in your life. Gratitude joins us with God and all creation and enables us to say "yes" to life and share our gifts with others.

pray

God of beauty and wonder, I thank you for the gifts of life.
I thank you for life-changing encounters, moments of grace,
times when I forgave and was forgiven,
for the gifts of others and their impact on my life.
For all that has been: Thank you!
From thanksgiving, let my life be a blessing to others,
a great "yes" to the world one moment and encounter at a time.
Amen.

act

Call a friend, parent, teacher, or colleague, and say thank you for their impact on your life. Do something unexpected to benefit another out of the abundance you have received.

A Heart Bursting with Gratitude
Colleen M. Arnold, MD

reflect

When the stress level and busyness in my life are high,
I don't always take time to thank God
for the daily gifts he gives me.
I zip through the day and crash into bed
without even acknowledging all I've been given.

pray

Dear God, fill my heart with gratitude and appreciation.
Help me remember that every day I wake up is a gift;
each night I fall asleep is a blessing.
All the meals I eat and personal interactions I experience
are opportunities to thank you.
Help me to be continuously conscious
of your kindness and generosity.
Amen.

act

Stop at each meal today and thank God for something specific
you've experienced in the preceding hour.

Give Thanks with a Grateful Heart
Patricia Breen

reflect

Gratitude is a spiritual practice that changes our littleness into abundance. It changes how we see our lives, situations, and experiences. We can always find something to be grateful for, even when life is hard or less than ideal.

pray

Dear Jesus,
take all that is in me
and pour it out in a sacrifice of gratitude.
Teach me that gratitude is a way
to always come close to and experience your presence.
Practicing gratitude is an opportunity
to name all the ways you love and bless me in my life.
Amen.

act

Set a timer for five or ten minutes. Begin to count and name all your blessings, all the things for which you are grateful, all the ways that God loves and cares for you.

Offer a Prayer of Gratitude

Shannon K. Evans

r e f l e c t

They say laughter is the best medicine, but we know gratitude is healing too. Today let us pray with grateful hearts for what we still need and for the blessings that already surround us.

p r a y

Generous God, thank you
for the wondrous life you have given me.
For even in the struggle,
grace abounds.
Even in the hard times,
I see evidence of your hand.
Thank you for my loved ones
who bring my life joy and connection.
Thank you for meaningful work
through which I can serve others.
Thank you for the home
of this earth
and the way it awes and comforts me.
I revel in your goodness today.
Amen.

a c t

Propose to keep your eyes open to God's gifts today, and let gratitude swell your heart.

Count Your Blessings

Christopher Heffron

reflect

God sends us blessings throughout the day, though we don't always recognize or appreciate them. In order to cultivate a gracious heart, let us first pray for openness.

pray

Dear God, your blessings take many shapes
but I do not always welcome them.
In the busyness of the day, give me eyes to see
the beauty around me and a heart that is open to its graces.
Let me share those blessings with those who have less.
Amen.

act

At the close of the day today, write down three blessings that lifted your spirits. Offer up this prayer again in thanks to a generous God who provided them.

Seeing God in the Little Things

Colleen M. Arnold, MD

reflect

It's easy to see God's glory in the big stuff. The crash of an ocean wave, a dramatic bolt of lightning, a double rainbow across the sky—all showcase God's power and make us take notice. But what about the small stuff? How often do we let the simple things amaze us?

pray

Dear God,
Help me see each blessing you put in my path today
and let me gather them in my mind like a bouquet.
Help me notice each tiny treasure: my child's toothless grin;
the busy spider in the corner; the meal I enjoy;
my coworker's kind encouragement.
These are all the work of your hands,
just as much as the crashing surf and the thunderstorm.
I don't want to miss them.
Amen.

act

Keep a list of the small miracles you experience today. Review the list at bedtime to remind yourself of God's goodness.

A Simple Thanks

Daniel Imwalle

reflect

We may say thank you to someone who holds a door open for us or to a waiter who brings us food in a restaurant. But what does expressing gratitude really mean? May this prayer of thanks help you celebrate the multitude of blessings God has given you.

pray

I've been given much, Lord,
through your profound
and radiant love and grace.
Whether in sharing delicious meals
with loved ones
or basking in the glory
of the natural world—
all provided by you—
I am blessed indeed.
For all that you've given,
I say with simplicity and sincerity,
"Thank you."

act

What is something in your daily life that you take for granted but that is actually a blessing from God? Offer up a quick thank-you note to our Heavenly Father.

Your Gratitude ABCs

Maureen O'Brien

r e f l e c t

We sometimes get so caught up in fear that it's hard to remember all we have to be grateful for, and yet there's an array of things— an abundance.

p r a y

God, I get so shut within the fear of the future,
or of making a mistake,
or not effectively meeting responsibilities,
that my days becomes stale.
But I can practice gratitude,
and like opening a window wide,
I'm refreshed by the softness of grace blowing in.

a c t

Write down a list of "Gratitude ABCs." What are you grateful for that begins with A? With B? Continue through the alphabet. Create even more lightness by asking a family member to join in.

joy and wonder.

Now Is the Day of Salvation

Bruce Epperly

reflect

The words of Psalm 118:24, "This is the day that the Lord has made; let us rejoice and be glad in it," frame the day with hope and possibility. They remind us that now is the only moment there is, and that in this holy moment—this day—we can choose love, truth, joy, and forgiveness. We can begin again as God's companions in healing the world. We can do something wonderful, as poet Mary Oliver counsels, with our one "wild and precious life."

pray

God of change and glory, God of time and space,
in this holy moment give to me your grace.
Let me live this moment with joy and affirmation.
Let me share love and create beauty for you and my kin,
human and nonhuman alike.
For this is the day that you have made
and I will rejoice and be glad in it.
Amen.

act

In this unique and unrepeatable day, pause to consider: What acts of kindness and love will you perform? In what ways will you celebrate the fact that you woke up this morning to a day of possibility and wonder? How will you bring joy to the world today? Take time today to do something beautiful and loving for God.

The Creative Spark

Julia Walsh, FSPA

reflect

From the mystery of black holes to the flight of the intricate bee hummingbird, expressions of God's creativity are everywhere. Evidence of this holy creativity is revealed in the uniqueness of every human and the countless shades of color in creation.

pray

Creator God, I know I am made in your image and likeness,
and that you are the great creator. I long to be closer to you,
and I want to know what it is like to cocreate with you.
Yet it can be difficult for me to sense my creativity
or foster my creative skills.
Whether I am making a meal or tending to my home,
may I work with you to create beauty, truth, and nourishment
for other creatures in my community.
Amen.

act

Set a timer for ten minutes. Next draw a circle or another shape and fill it in with doodles and colors—no particular pattern or design is needed. At the end of the ten minutes write a poem describing what emerged in your creation.

Thin Places Everywhere

Bruce Epperly

reflect

Celtic Christians spoke of "thin places" as locations where heaven and earth meet. While certain places may be set apart as revealing God, all places reflect God's presence. Every place is a gateway to heaven.

pray

God of insight and revelation,
open my senses to your presence in all things.
Help me to see you in unexpected places
and bring forth beauty where others see ugliness.
Let me dwell in your glory and love.

act

Notice "thin places" today. Keep your eyes open to unexpected beauty and, if appropriate, share these experiences with others.

Perfect Joy

Christopher Heffron

r e f l e c t

With the health crises, war, violence, and unrest facing our world, finding a reason to be joyful is hard. But it's important that we smile—even if it's through tears.

p r a y

Dear God,
Sadness surrounds us
and for that I haven't much reason
to be joyful.
But my battered heart longs
for a moment of joy.
Remind me that,
though our spirits are wounded,
above the heavy clouds is the sun
waiting to warm us.
After the storm passes,
I know I will see clear skies.
That alone is reason to smile.
Amen.

a c t

Do one thing today that makes you feel better. Rise above the storm of grief—if only for a moment—and give yourself permission to be happy.

Finding Joy in Challenging Times
Bruce Epperly

reflect

St. Paul, writing from prison to the first-century church
in Philippi, proclaims, "Rejoice, again, I say rejoice." Paul's
affirmation challenges us to ask: Can you have joy in a difficult
time? Can you experience wonder and beauty, and rejoice in
a time of pandemic? For Paul, joy is not accidental, but the
result of prayers of gratitude and petition, kindness to others,
contemplation, and trusting that in all things God is your
companion. Out of our joy, we can be a blessing to others.

pray

God of all seasons, I give thanks for your presence.
Thank you for waking me up to a day of possibility and adventure.
Thank you for the blessings of friendship.
Let me trust you with life's challenges,
knowing that your love will get me through
and that you will make a way where I perceive no way.
Help me be joyful and share my joy with others.
Amen.

act

Joy is a relational virtue. Trusting God's presence and care, take
time to reach out to another. Have as your intention the desire
to do something that will bring joy and comfort to them. Be a joy-
bringer, adding to the well-being of those around you.

Time to Play

Susan Hines-Brigger

reflect

Do you remember the joy you felt when you were younger and how much fun you would have running around outside and playing with your friends? When was the last time you did something that brought you that same feeling of joy? Just because we grow older, we don't have to lose that sense of adventure and fun.

pray

Lord, inspire me to, once again, seek out and embrace
the many joys that life has to offer.
Help me remember to embrace and celebrate the beauty of life.

act

Schedule a date to get together with friends and do something fun.

Small Treats
Bruce Epperly

reflect

Philosopher Iris Murdoch stated that "one of the secrets to a happy life is continuous small treats." God brought wonder, beauty, and joy to the world. What other treats fill your day? Which of your treats do you share with others?

pray

Thank you, Bountiful Creator, for the wonders of life,
for small things that shape a great life,
for the simple joys of each day,
for treats that enliven the spirit.
Let the joy I feel in living each day flood into the world,
adding zest and beauty to my relationships,
and inviting others to delight in this unrepeatable day.

act

What small treat can you reward yourself with today? What treat can you share with another person?

A World of Praise

Bruce Epperly

reflect

Psalm 148—like Francis of Assisi's "Canticle of the Creatures"—
describes a world of praise. To the psalmist, everything from
frost and hail to political leaders praises God. The psalms end
with, "Let everything that breathes, praise God! Praise God!" You
are a member in God's chorus of praise. Let your voice join the
anthem of creation.

pray

Let my life give you praise, Joyful Creator.
Let my words, acts, and commitments bring joy to the world.
Let me experience praise everywhere
and let me bring praise to every situation.
Delighting in the wonder of your loving artistry,
let me be a poet of creation and bard of the spirit,
bringing delight to your glorious world.
Amen.

act

What song or hymn captures the meaning of praise for you? Sing
that song throughout the day today, letting your voice brighten
the world and awaken your senses to the wonders of God's love.

Do the Joy

Daniel Imwalle

reflect

Most people would say that they want to be happy. But what about being joyful? Happiness may feel good in the moment, but it inevitably fades and disappears. Joy is something we can experience in the long-term. We need only to let God into our hearts.

pray

I'm tired, God,
of chasing after what's promised
to bring me happiness,
but which seems
to slip through my fingers
once I possess it.
Instead, I invite you into my heart
to fill my soul
with that deep, abiding joy
only you can offer.
I will radiate your joy
to those around me
and proclaim your name.
Amen.

act

Joy isn't passive, but rather an outward and active way of glorifying God. What is something that you can rejoice in today?

Hello, Joy!
Maureen O'Brien

reflect

Think about letting go a bit. When was the last time you let yourself be silly, play around, be goofy? As children, we did this freely and without hesitation. Can you use the word *joy* more often in your everyday life?

pray

Today I long to take a breather from the constant focus on the "have-tos," the "to-do list," the weekly calendar, the monthly bills, the daily chores and reminders.
I know I can stay on task
and yet also greet more joy on this journey.
This is your will for me, to give and receive joy, to fully blossom.
Can I be less serious, less fretful, open to more fullness
in the perfect rays of your unfailing love?
Help me to hold back nothing.

act

There are times we just need to let down our pride and dance—right now, right here. Today, let the kid inside you whirl around for a while.

care for creation.

Honor Creation with Integrity

Shannon K. Evans

reflect

St. Francis of Assisi taught that in God we are connected to the earth and all created things. In the spiritual life we are called to live attuned to this interdependence in small but important ways.

pray

Creator of heaven and earth,
Today I remember
the many small ways
I can honor the divine life
all around me.
As I reach down to pick up trash
from the sidewalk
or move a bug outdoors
instead of killing it,
may your Spirit fill me
with the knowledge
that all things
are my brothers and sisters.
Amen.

act

Choose one simple way that you can begin to honor creation with more integrity. Ideas might include starting a compost pile, locating and using a recycling site, joining a farm co-op, or mending clothes instead of discarding them.

God's Song

Christopher Heffron

reflect

Do you ever slow down long enough to admire the world around you? God gave it to us to protect and appreciate. Do you see it?

pray

Dear God, the leaves on the trees sway to the
rhythm of your song.
The birds are singing your chorus while the breeze
holds the melody.
Let me stop and appreciate your symphony.
And let me add my own notes.
For I am an instrument—
and together we are an interconnected part
of your majesty,
your gifts,
this world,
our home.
Amen.

act

It's hard to appreciate the natural world from inside. If you can, take a walk and immerse yourself in the wonders of our planet. You'll find God there.

Signs of Spring
Shannon K. Evans

reflect

As the world around us thaws and blossoms, new truths about
God catch our attention in everyday ways.

pray

Giver of life, I see you in the earth you so lovingly made;
the earth that mirrors the gospel of life, death, and resurrection.
Thank you for this most special season of spring,
when I am reminded of your promise that death is not the end
and nothing lasts forever.
Grant me the grace to believe that
though seasons of harsh winter and hardship last for a while,
they do not last forever.
As the world around me re-enlivens,
may I cling to the promise that so too will my soul.
Amen.

act

If conditions allow, sit or take a walk outside and observe the
changes brought by spring. Let your observation be a prayer that
points your soul back to resurrection.

A Testament to God's Majesty

Clifford Hennings, OFM

reflect

Nature attests to the majesty of its author, if we have the eyes to see and ears to listen. Give God thanks for our ability to study the sciences, grateful for our intellect, and the workings of the world.

pray

Lord, all creation proclaims your glory.
All beauty proclaims your love.
You have made us in your image,
able to understand the inner workings of the world.
May our sciences reveal your wonders
in a spirit of humility and awe.
May our knowledge work for the good of all,
and not for ill.
Amen.

act

Throughout the day today, pay attention to the marvels of modern science that we often take for granted.

Whatever the Weather

Shannon K. Evans

reflect

The weather can have a direct affect on our mental and emotional
well-being. But when we choose to see our connection to
the created world, we can be sure that—rain or shine—we will
encounter the sacred.

pray

God of warm summer nights
and freezing gray mornings,
help me respond to the invitation of the earth today.
Whether in boundless energy
or in contemplative stillness,
may I accept and not judge
my body's response to the weather.
May I recognize that everything has its place,
and everything has its time—
including my feelings.
Amen.

act

Check the weather forecast for today. Think of how you can use
the weather to draw near, listen, and respond to God's voice.

Bless Our Pets

Daniel Imwalle

reflect

We often get swept up in the daily chores that come with pet ownership, whether it's taking the dog for a walk, cleaning the cat litter, or feeding the fish. But if you're a proud "parent" of a pet or have a "granddog" in your life, you give thanks that their enriching presence is a reflection of God's love.

pray

God of creation, you have blessed us with the
companionship of not only our human friends
and family, but also our animal friends.
Many of us count them as family,
and they bring countless moments of both joy and solace.
Whether they are canine, feline, have scales,
or wear feathers, they all come from you.
We thank you for the warmth of their presence in our lives and
humbly accept the responsibility to be their caretakers on earth.
Amen.

act

If you have a pet, take a moment to let your animal companion know that you love him or her. If you don't, why not bring a small treat the next time you visit with a pet owner? Although they can't say thank you in human language, they know they are loved and relish the love shown to them.

Prayer Birds

Maureen O'Brien

reflect

Listen to the sounds of nature in your world—the swoosh of leaves, the bend of branches. Stop and listen, even if you are in a parking lot or on a city street. There's beauty everywhere, calling to you.

pray

Morning birds, let me hear you.
Morning birds, you, too, must know God,
because you begin to call out
the precise moment that night tips toward day.
You're the first to declare the end of the darkness has begun.
Morning birds, I can't always see you there,
but you connect everything with your songs,
reminding us how we are together in this world.
Morning birds, you sing for us all—
the raindrops beginning to tap upon the window,
the underside of leaves swishing, flipping open in the wind.

act

Today before checking your email, your phone, and connecting with the outer world, start your day noticing the simple, nearby joys already here.

Keeping Our World Beautiful
Daniel Imwalle

reflect

Nature is one of God's greatest gifts. Yet we treat it with such disregard and disrespect that one day in the not-too-distant future, the world will become an unlivable place. May we pray for a healthier planet for future generations to enjoy.

pray

Dear God,
please forgive us
for our treatment
of this beautiful world,
which you have
so graciously
given to us to watch over
as devoted stewards.
Give us the strength
to seek new ways
to protect your wondrous creation.
Lead us with the light
of your love.
Amen.

act

Identify one way you can help protect the environment, whether it be donating to a conservational charity or giving up the use of plastic straws.

Cycles of Creation

Natalie Ryan

reflect

The seasons contain life, death, and transformation. Crisp, cold air rushes through the bare limbs and over the powdered snow. In time, these limbs begin to bud, the white melts into browns and greens. Flowers bloom. Leaves wave in the summer breeze as the animals scurry along. Soon enough, the earth broadens its color palette to range from light greens to mustard yellows to blood red to rusty oranges—only to return to cold air once again. God sets all in motion.

pray

Lord, your creation holds so much life.
Thank you for the many lessons nature gives us.
In everything, there is a season—
a different color, a different feeling, a different task.
You, Lord, show your reflection like a mirror in creation.
You, Lord, are in it all.
Amen.

act

Take a walk outside today and admire the beauty. Where do you see God in nature around you?

Mindful Eating

Bond Strong

r e f l e c t

Wendell Berry—Kentucky farmer, writer, and activist—said, "Eating is an agricultural act." It is also a spiritual act. How, when, what, and why, are questions that, when asked about our food and eating, can transform a necessary and habitual act into a form of resistance, love, and even prayer.

p r a y

God, who gave us plants and animals to eat and water to drink,
who instituted an edible sacrament,
reveal to us the power of the act.
Help us to make wise decisions around our food,
honoring your creation and ultimate plan.
Amen.

a c t

Support your neighbor and encourage sustainability by buying ingredients for a meal from a local farmer.

love.

A Gospel Summary in Four Words
Patricia Breen

reflect

Love God. Love neighbor. The fulfillment of the Old Testament
that Jesus embodied is revealed in these four words—a most
striking summary of the Gospel. Sometimes we overcomplicate
things when it comes to faith, God, and spirituality. However, this
gospel summary reminds us that love of God and love of neighbor
are what matters most.

pray

Dear Jesus,
teach me to love you
above all things
and to love my neighbor
as myself.
Show me what it means
to truly live the gospel message
in these powerful words.
Help me be your hands, feet,
and presence in the world
to all those I encounter.
Amen.

act

Who is my neighbor? How am I called to love him or her today?

Beloved Child

Stephen Copeland

r e f l e c t

We often go to God in prayer, but do we ever allow God to pray over us? May this prayer inspire your Christian imagination to experience the intimate grace that perpetually washes over us every day. May it baptize you with the truth of God's love.

p r a y

I know sometimes you slip into lies
you've believed.
I know sometimes old ways return,
forgetting love you have received.
I know sometimes
you have better days.
I know sometimes
you lose touch with grace.
But did you know I love you still,
that you're mine and mine alone?
Did you know I will not leave you,
my beloved child?

a c t

In the morning, afternoon, and evening today, enter into stillness and be reminded that God dwells within you—in the deepest levels of your being—and animates you through the mystery of the Holy Spirit. Come home to this truth and allow God to pray over you.

Just Knock
Natalie Ryan

reflect

God already knows the desires of our hearts, but he wants us to ask. Our loved ones know that we love them, but it feels good to hear and to say. God enjoys our heart-to-heart conversations with him too.

pray

Lord of all creation, thank you for this day
and all you have given us.
You see me. You hear me.
You know what's on my heart.
You're here with me.
I lift my intentions to you.
Amen.

act

Lay down your fears, burdens, questions, and intentions at his feet. Just ask God.

Loved into Existence

Stephen Copeland

reflect

Poet John O'Donohue once wrote, "I would love to live like a river flows, carried by the surprise of its own unfolding." May this prayer heighten your awareness of the divine flow of your life and your ongoing dance with the Trinity.

pray

What a miracle it is to be loved into existence,
even now, wherever I am, still in this moment,
no matter what has led me here,
no matter my inner or outer state—
the length of the night, the noise of the day—
I am reminded I am enough
as you fill my lungs and bring me to life,
as you flow through my being.
Trinity, help me flow as you flow
out of the infinite well of love within
as I am loved by you in this very moment,
this unfolding miracle, this ever-flowing love.

act

Every time you catch yourself bored with life or going through the motions, consider reciting a phrase from this prayer to heighten your awareness for the miracle of being loved into existence, just as you are.

Created for Connection

Shannon K. Evans

reflect

Every human being needs camaraderie and friendship. We are simply not made to walk alone. But it's all too easy to fail to reach out for connection when we need it most. May this prayer compel you toward communion with another.

pray

Holy Trinity,
you have not created me
for loneliness or disconnection.
I confess my need
for my fellow human beings,
knowing they have so often been
your tangible presence in my life.
God of communion,
give me the wherewithal
to reach out
to a friend today
and find the connection
my heart needs.
Amen.

act

Think of one friend you would like to connect with this week. Contact them today and make a plan to have a long conversation, either in person or over the phone, in the next few days.

There Is One Who Loves All of Me

Vanesa Zuleta Goldberg

reflect

We are always working to be good enough. Good enough for our family, for our marriage, for our friends, for the world around us. Yet, when God created us he not only knew we were wholly good, but he reveled in it: "And God knew that this was very good" (Genesis 1:31).

pray

To the one who loves all of me,
may I come to know deeply
the breath of life that you shared with me.
May I come to know your love that draws me,
whole as I am,
closer to your heart.
May the lies of the world hold no claim over me.
May I know that to you, I am good.
Amen.

act

Today, pray with the truth that you are good, and that God calls you to participate in his goodness every day.

Show Me How to Love You

Shannon K. Evans

reflect

Sometimes the flame of our love for God grows dim. It is then that we must return to the small ways God woos us in everyday life. Our prayer is this...

pray

Holy God, make yourself known to me

in the flames of a fire that gives me warmth,

in the smile of a baby that brings me joy,

in the touch of a friend that reminds me that I am not alone.

Captivate me in the mundane so I may return to you

the love you so lavishly pour on me.

Amen.

act

Be alert to the many ways the Spirit of God is wanting to enchant you today. Allow your heart to respond with love back to God.

Spread Some Love

Susan Hines-Brigger

reflect

All too often people view love through the narrow lens of romance. The truth is, though, love is so much broader than that. It can take on so many different forms and be expressed in so many different ways. We just need to broaden our lens.

pray

Dear God,
you showed us your love
by your ultimate sacrifice
on the cross.
Help us to open our eyes
to the many ways
we ourselves
can bring love
to a world
desperately in need.
And may we remember
that your second greatest
commandment is to love others.
Amen.

act

Find a way that you can show your love for others. Remember that sometimes even the smallest of gestures can have the greatest impact.

Staying Close

Natalie Ryan

reflect

Elijah heard God in the simplest whisper, not in the cataclysmic, earth-shattering events. One can witness a storm, a fire, an earthquake from far away and see their impact. One can only hear a whisper if the speaker is close.

pray

All-powerful God, you are so close,
you never leave my side.
Attune my ears to hear your words,
even the slightest of whispers.
I feel your proximity, I feel your gentle nudge,
I feel your warm hug, I feel your comforting hand.
You are with me today, tomorrow, and always.
Amen.

act

Read the story of Elijah in 1 Kings 19:11–21 and put yourself in Elijah's shoes (or sandals?). How is God moving you? How do you respond to God's voice?

Our Blessed Little Flower

Maureen O'Brien

reflect

Honor St. Thérèse by thinking of all the small things you do to try
to be the best and most loving person you can be: starting the day
with prayer; listening patiently to another's woes; letting another
car go ahead of you. All these things count, and all are beautiful.

pray

How blessed we are to have you, St. Thérèse,
to show us that tiny things have magnitude in God's eyes.
Like you, I feel small.
Thank you for pointing me to what really matters:
the love.
St. Thérèse, thank you for living a life
ever-present to the possibility of bringing your love
to the ordinary and the routine.
It's enough for any of us to be one sweet blossom,
petite-petaled.

act

Today, feel the humility and truth of St. Thérèse of Lisieux's
words: "Always doing the smallest right and doing it all for love."

family.

Praying for Our Families

Christopher Heffron

reflect

Family can take many forms—beyond our blood relatives. Family can also encompass friends, neighbors, and coworkers. Now is a good time to pray for those whom we call family.

pray

Dear God, life can be a challenge,
but you've surrounded me with
people who warm my heart
and nurture my spirit.
Keep them safe and sound in your loving care.
Let me never forget that family, whatever shape it takes,
is a ready source of warmth when I am cold.
Amen.

act

Share this prayer with a friend or family member who needs it most.

Being a Family
Susan Hines-Brigger

reflect

Family life can play out in so many different ways. It can be joyful, stressful, chaotic, sad, and many other emotions. At the heart of each family, however, is love—even if at times it gets buried underneath the messiness of life. We must continue to uncover that love for each other every day.

pray

Dear God, may our family recognize
the blessing that we are to each other.
Help us to remember that we are stronger
when we come together
and weaker when we allow ourselves to drift apart.
Let us come together and share our unique
strengths and gifts
for the good of our family.
Amen.

act

Plan a family dinner soon so that everyone can come together and talk with each other. Come up with some conversation starter questions to help get discussions going.

The Good and Bad Days of Family

Vanesa Zuleta Goldberg

reflect

Families are complex. We have good days and bad days.
St. Joseph reminds us that the calling to be a father, mother,
son, or daughter is a calling from God that draws us into a
life-giving relationship with others.

pray

St. Joseph, earthly father of Christ, husband of Mother Mary,
through your intercession we ask God to bless our families.
May you intercede on our behalf on the good and the bad days.
May you lift our prayers to your Son, Jesus,
and keep us close to his heart and yours.
Amen.

act

Make time today to sit with one of your family members and ask
how they are doing. Share with them the joys and trials of your
day, and make space to do the same for them, always reminding
them of your love.

Wisdom Comes from Age

Shannon K. Evans

reflect

Our elders have important wisdom to offer us, but many are suffering as well. Let us pray for the elderly people we know that we may receive their gifts and alleviate their burdens.

pray

O God Eternal, may my ears listen
to the wisdom of my elders,
and may my arms uphold them
in their times of grief or pain.
I recognize the holiness of a long life
and pray a blessing of peace
and a community of love
for all those older than myself.
Amen.

act

Whatever your age, you likely know someone who is older. Reach out to them today through a visit or a phone call, and ask thoughtful questi

God Bless Fathers

Christopher Heffron

reflect

Fathers have no better role model than St. Joseph, who exhibited a kind of quiet strength that is essential within a family dynamic.

pray

Dear God,
I thank you
for the strength and support
of loving dads everywhere.
You entrusted your Son to St. Joseph,
who raised him,
loved him,
and emboldened him
to begin his ministry.
May all fathers feel called to model
that same kind of selfless love.
Amen.

act

Share this prayer with a father who emulates the same characteristics as St. Joseph. A prayerful word of thanks is always the best present.

God Bless Mothers

Christopher Heffron

reflect

When we're down, regardless of our age, we seek the solace of our mothers. They model a kind of love that is boundless and pure.

pray

Dear God,
Mothers are instruments of compassion, as you
showed us with Mary, our universal mother.
My own mom is far less famous, much less revered,
though no less loved.
Thank you for mothers everywhere
who give love and support
and want nothing in return.
Such a love can only come from you,
a loving God.
Amen.

act

A call, a card, a text, a visit: Reach out to your mom today. If she's no longer with us, spend a moment in prayer for the woman who loved you first—and loved you most.

Our Unbreakable Bonds

Daniel Imwalle

r e f l e c t

Despite our differences, we are profoundly connected by family.
We may have arguments and even take time apart to heal,
but the core of family life is rooted in love. We can look to our
faith to remind us that family goes far deeper than the image
in commercials and on billboards. A loving family reflects and
demonstrates the infinite love God has in store for us.

p r a y

Loving God, help me to continually remember
the presence and power of family in my life.
Whether it be someone living or a loved one who has passed,
may I embrace that connection and offer up
a word of thanks and praise for having known him or her.
Where there is brokenness in my family,
I ask that you shine your healing light in those places.
Where there is happiness and wholeness,
may I be grateful and appreciative.
No matter where life takes me,
may I always bring my love of family along in my heart.

a c t

Family might mean different things to different people. Take
a moment to think of someone from your "work family" or your
"family of friends." Let that person know who she or he is for you.
They may be surprised and almost certainly delighted.

Gifted with Siblings

Shannon K. Evans

reflect

Our brothers and sisters can be some of the greatest blessings in our life, but they can also cause pain. Whichever reality we are experiencing right now, God desires to listen and be present to our needs, hopes, hurts, and concerns for our siblings.

pray

Dear God, I know you love my siblings even more than I do,
and you are active in their lives.
I pray that you will comfort and strengthen them
in precisely the way they need it today.
Keep them from feeling alone or abandoned
and let them experience your nearness in a healing way.
Help me to support and love them in ways they can best receive.
Help me stay true to myself
while caring for this person I love deeply.
Show me what their needs are
and how I can be Christ to them today.

act

Reach out to your siblings through a phone call, email, or written letter, simply to let them know that you love and care for them.

Be a Good Ancestor
Bruce Epperly

reflect
___

Each moment provides the opportunity to be God's companion
in creating a positive future. When we look beyond ourselves and
act with concern for future generations, our actions will outlive
us. They may even turn the tide of history from death to life.
Each action matters. Live as if this present moment shapes the
destiny of the planet. Let God's love flow through you to people
you will never meet.

pray
___

O God, our help in ages past and hope in years to come,
help me to see each moment as holy—
as an opportunity to share your love right now
and shape the future in ways I cannot imagine.
Let me bring peace on earth and good will to all.

act
___

Be mindful of your interactions today. Enjoy the day, rejoice in its
beauty, and add beauty to the world one act at a time. Who needs
your love today? Where might your compassion tip the balance
from hate to love, and from death to life in this moment, for you
and for those who follow you?

Worried for Your Family?

Maureen O'Brien

reflect

In my worry about family members, I sometimes forget that there is always hope—in God. Are there moments you feel you must fix things, forgetting that God is there?

pray

Sometimes I am overwrought about members of my family—
so worried that they are lost in their inward hurting.
Help me trust that you have them in your sight.
You are the shepherd.
You adore each and every one of us.
Though I am limited in what I can do,
I can hold my loved ones in my heart
and know that you are there alongside them,
filling their emptiness with your overflowing love.
And I pray that they can feel it.

act

Read Psalm 23 out loud—several times if needed—and think both of yourself and your loved one being guided. See if you can let the beauty of the psalm "restore" you, to wash away your worry.

Praying the Pictures
Carol Ann Morrow

reflect

Home is not complete without a few frames of Mom and Dad,
family vacation poses, and refrigerator magnets from little
scholars year after year. Looking at them can inspire memories—
and more.

pray

While I gaze at the cross
and remember all that you have done for me—
Jesus, Son of God—I have no photos.
Help me see you in the photos I do have.
I praise you for the gift of Mom and Dad,
their smiles captured in this frame.
Thank you for allowing us to see your beautiful world
and revealing it anew in this image
of the ocean waves' embrace.
May my memories of kindergarten, diplomas, and weddings
be dust-free today.
No glass can block me from these many gifts
from you, Great Family of Three.

act

It may take several days to see the divine image in every framed
photo or crinkled headshot carried in cracked plastic in a billfold
or tiny album. But when you do, offer a thanksgiving for each
loved one in God's family.

God Does Not Hate Divorced People

Patricia Breen

reflect

Sometimes life goes much differently than we hope for or imagine. Divorce is one of those painful experiences many of us do not anticipate will touch our personal lives. Realizing that divorce is never an easy decision—even if it is the right one—God does not hate divorced people or the choices they feel they have to make.

pray

Dear God,
the pain of divorce was never a part of your original plan.
And yet sometimes, it is in the messiest and painful places
that you come close and bring about healing and transformation.
Please bless and watch over families, parents, and children
struggling through a divorce.
May you be their peace and comfort amid the storm.
Amen.

act

Is there a friend, coworker, or family member you are close to who is navigating the pain of divorce in their life? Reach out to him or her and ask how you can best love and support them in this difficult time.

sorrow and grief.

Some Days It's Hard to Get Out of Bed

Colleen M. Arnold, MD

reflect

Some mornings you wake up dreading the day ahead. Whether it's the thought of an unpleasant confrontation, a physically demanding task, or just low energy from an overstressed life, sometimes it's hard to get going.

pray

Dear God, be with me today in all I think, say, and do.
Give my hands the strength and skill I need.
Give my heart the love and compassion I need.
Give my head the wisdom and knowledge I need.
Help me accomplish whatever lies ahead of me
and remind me throughout the day that you are there.
Amen.

act

Picture God with you in the difficult part of your day, helping it to go smoothly.

Mercy in the Midst of Melancholy

Daniel Imwalle

reflect

As hard as it is to cope with, sadness is a part of life and a hidden opportunity to get closer to God. In our sorrows we are brought into solidarity with Jesus, who wept bitterly in the Garden of Gethsemane. May this prayer about sadness bring you some light in the darkness you are experiencing.

pray

Dear Lord,
tears are streaming
down my face
and I feel alone,
separate from you
and from those I love.
Only your love and mercy
can turn this sorrow
into strength.
I pray to you
to reach into
the broken places
in my heart
and mend them.
Amen.

act

What causes you sadness? Meditate on how your suffering is not meaningless, but rather a tool for cultivating compassion.

Do You Ever Feel Abandoned?

Herman Sutter

reflect

When bad things happen to us we often wonder why God didn't protect us. In Psalm 80, Israel asks that same question. God brought Israel out of Egypt, planted it like a vine, but just as she began to thrive, everything changed. Every bird of the air and beast of the forest (think of Babylon and Assyria) was plucking her fruit and ravaging the vine. Why? Where is God when we are feeling abandoned?

pray

Dear Lord, like your Son on the cross,
sometimes I feel abandoned.
And yet I know you are always with me,
as you were with him on the darkest of days.
Grant me the courage to trust you, completely,
faithfully, gratefully.
Let my prayer be only this: Thy will be done.

act

Offer a brief prayer of thanks that God is with us always, especially when we feel abandoned. After praying, think of those who feel abandoned by our society. Take note that your prayer brings you into solidarity with those on the margins.

Gather the Fragments

Maureen O'Brien

reflect

In the multiplication of the loaves miracle, Jesus fed the crowd, and when there was bread left over he instructed, "Gather the fragments." Think of aspects of your past that can still be healed.

pray

God, if I think about those three words,
they call forth all the pieces of dreams I lost,
scattered behind me.
If I turn around and look, those shards
still seem to cut me.
But you teach me that no matter my heartache,
you hold it with me—for me.
When I let you gather all that has been broken,
I feel how your peace restores me,
making me whole.

act

Today, envision giving Jesus your regrets and sorrows of the past. Imagine him gathering the fragments and cradling them so that your heart, in this present moment, can let go and sing and be free.

Body and Spirit
Christopher Heffron

reflect

For those who suffer from chronic illness, every day can be a challenge. Even the simplest tasks require a monumental effort. If you suffer in body, know that God is with you in spirit.

pray

God of wholeness,
pain is my constant companion—
so much so that I struggle to find a moment of respite.
Grant that I may find relief in your company.
Bless my broken body and give me the strength
to greet the day with peace of mind.
All strength, all wellness, all comfort comes from you.
Amen.

act

Close your eyes and spend a moment in stillness. Pray for those who are sick. If you are well, share this prayer with those whose spirits could use a lift.

Alone or Lonely?

Carol Ann Morrow

reflect

Jesus was alone in the desert for forty days. Unless I am aware of the world through media or the nearby presence of another, being alone can be too difficult, even impossible to sustain.

Pray

I believe that I am in the presence of the Divine.
I am not alone.
In times of isolation or illness,
this can be hard to remember.
Longing for a comforting glance
or a word of recognition is natural,
even for those who embrace solitude.
Such comfort is not always close at hand.
Accept my pain, my panic, my desire to reach out,
O Lover of my soul.
Help me to rest in your invisible embrace.

Act

Today, I will choose—not just accept—a few moments of alone time. I will acknowledge that God is within and without. I will strengthen my ability to embrace the loneliness I do not choose.

They Are Always with Us

Colleen M. Arnold, MD

reflect

Losing someone we love is difficult. Even though we believe in heaven and life after death, their absence from everyday life is painful.

pray

Dear Lord, you put people in my life, and then you take them away.
Oh, how my heart struggles with that!
I know I will see them again, but sometimes that isn't enough.
Please help me feel their presence;
remind me that those I love are always with me
and the moments we've shared
are part of the person I have become.
Amen.

act

Find a picture of someone you love who has died. As you look at it, spend five minutes remembering ways that they impacted your life and helped you become a better person.

Your Grief Matters

Shannon K. Evans

r e f l e c t

Grief can take many forms and be triggered by losses both big and small. May this prayer offer comfort in your process of grieving.

p r a y

God of all comfort,
my pain is unique
and it is real.
Sometimes I feel
so alone in my grief,
but I know that you have never left me.
Help me receive your care
and feel the comfort of your arms
until my pain recedes
and the day is made new.
Amen.

a c t

Set aside time today to express your grief. It might feel good to journal, cry, scream, or punch a pillow. Remember that your pain is valid and deserves to be given a voice in a safe and healthy way.

A Heart Not Only Broken, but Open

Daniel Imwalle

reflect

Grief over the death of a loved one is one of the sharpest pains the human heart can feel. God's love for us and those we have lost is the healing light we need to see the way forward.

pray

Dear God,
I have a dull, aching pain in my heart
that sometimes swells with sadness.
I get a knot in my throat,
and then the tears begin—again.
I've lost someone dear to me,
and now my despair feels deeper than ever.
I know I'll never "get over" this loss,
but I humbly ask you to help guide me through grief
to a place of understanding and acceptance.
May I take comfort that my loved one is with you,
and you are with me.
Amen.

act

Take a moment and think of one way you brought joy to a loved one who has passed away. Recognize the inherent good of that word or deed and offer up a quick thank-you to God for having been able to experience it.

Grieving Under Empty Skies

Maureen O'Brien

reflect

Grief cannot be outrun. Let this prayer both honor your mourning
and remind you of the joy in God's heart.

pray

God, I am bent by the weight of this grief—
the loss of my loved one.
I carry it everywhere I go, day and night.
But when I remember those moments of delight,
recalling when we laughed together,
the burden of their loss is not as heavy,
though my still heart beats alone without them here.
And so as I am lighter, able to look up into the still-empty sky,
I pray for them, knowing they have flown toward joy:
now held within the freedom and beauty
of your loving Sacred Heart.

act

Find an image of the Sacred Heart of Jesus. As you think of
your lost loved one, imagine connecting the light from Jesus'
heart to yours. Allow yourself to experience the full range of your
emotions.

The Silent Sisterhood

Richard Patterson

reflect

There are many women who suffer silently over the loss of a child through illness, accident, miscarriage, or abortion. They may stay silent long after the event has passed, yet they still grieve. We may know such women, but we don't know what to say, and so we just encourage them to get on with their lives.

pray

Lord, please comfort the women in my life
who have suffered the loss of a child.
You also grieve over their tragic losses.
Help them feel your presence
and reassure them that their child has gone before them
to prepare a place.

act

If you are one of the "silent sisterhood," share your grief with God, perhaps by writing a letter to God and one to the child you lost. If you know other recent members of the "silent sisterhood," reach out to them, letting your own experience be a reassurance to them that they, too, can heal.

Reminders of Life

Natalie Ryan

reflect

After losing someone, I wish desperately to be able to pick up the phone to call them, to hear their voice. I can at least see their face in pictures. Remembering all of the happy and funny memories from over the years makes my heart twinkle with light. When the world seems to be dark, stagnant, numb, and lonely, memory plays such an important role in bringing the light back.

pray

Lord, enter my heart, invoke my memory.
When my faith is bland,
when my prayer life seems nonexistent, remind me.
Remind me of when my soul first met you,
when in a moment everything changed.
Everything filled with warmth, peace, joy.
Enlighten my mind and soothe my heart.
Amen.

act

Recall a moment when you had some kind of enlightenment or spiritual conversion. Sit with the details, the feelings, and the memory of Jesus meeting you where you are.

forgiveness.

Forgiveness 101

Patricia Breen

reflect

Forgiveness is one of the most foundational teachings of Christian theology. However, it is one of the most difficult to live out and practice in our daily lives. Two ways to grow in the way of forgiveness are grace and desire.

pray

Jesus, our brother, pour out your grace on me
to help forgive those who wrong me.
I cannot do it on my own and need your help.
When it is most difficult, help me to ask you
to give me the desire to forgive, even if I would rather not.
You modeled forgiveness from the cross; help me
become more like you.
Amen.

act

Are there people in your life you find it difficult to forgive? Ask Jesus to send you grace and give you the desire.

Past Hurts, Future Hopes
Bruce Epperly

reflect

In letting go of the past through prayer, meditation, spiritual direction, or counseling, you can begin anew. You can be reconciled in spirit, even if you are unable to forgive in person. You can experience a lightness of being that opens you to God's vision of the future.

pray

God of every tomorrow,
fill me with your love.
Open me to new life.
Help me to let go of the past
and open to the future you plan for me.
Touch me with the gift of healing
as I place my grievances in your hand.
Heal my heart
and fill me with your love.
Be with me as I begin again
so that my life will be a blessing to others.
Amen.

act

Forgiveness is an inner journey before it becomes an external action. If you cannot yet forgive another person, seek the help of a trained pastor, counselor, or spiritual director. Place persons you cannot forgive in God's care, knowing that God loves you even if you cannot forgive. Leave the forgiveness to God.

Learning to Forgive

Shannon K. Evans

reflect

When we are wronged, offering forgiveness is not often our natural response. Yet God asks us to forgive—not for empty piety, but to help our souls heal. May this prayer aid you in the work of your heart.

pray

Holy Spirit, be a comforter in my wounded places.
Where I have been painfully wronged
grant me the grace to extend forgiveness.
Help me create the boundaries I need to continue to love
without allowing myself to be hurt in the same way again.
I pray I may be whole and free and able to forgive.
Amen.

act

Who do you need to forgive? Use this prayer to help you extend forgiveness while discerning what the repaired relationship might look like.

Praying with Bakhita
Christopher Heffron

reflect

St. Josephine Bakhita bore scars throughout her body from years of slavery, yet her courageous heart remained unblemished. She forgave her enslavers because she understood something they could not: Love will always conquer hate.

pray

Dear God,
Josephine Bakhita endured horrors
I cannot fathom,
yet her bravery,
her mercy,
and her warrior spirit
could not be restrained
by man-made chains.
Teach me to forgive as she forgave
and to love as she loved.
Help me to understand
what she understood with such clarity:
True freedom can only come
from you.
Amen.

act

Visit SaintoftheDay.org to learn more about the life and legacy of St. Josephine. Share her story so that others may be inspired by this remarkable woman.

What Comes after Forgiveness?
Shannon K. Evans

reflect

Forgiveness is an important part of spiritual health, but appropriate boundaries can be equally as important when the offense was significant. Here is a prayer for discerning what to do after forgiving someone who deeply hurt you.

pray

O Great Reconciler,
I have chosen to forgive the person who hurt me,
so that I may be free from bitterness.
Now light my way and show me how
to move forward in freedom and love,
without permitting the continuation
of any form of abuse.
Give me clarity and peace to discern
what healthy forgiveness looks like
in this particular moment.
Amen.

act

Find a resource to help you navigate this relationship after extending forgiveness. A book or podcast by a professional counselor might be helpful, or you might benefit from making an appointment with a therapist.

Riverbank of Love

Maureen O'Brien

reflect

When you wake up off-kilter, notice how your thoughts take you in the wrong direction. Some of the harshest criticisms are those leveled at ourselves. Know that God will try to guide you back.

pray

What harsh river of dreams swept me away last night
and led me to this?
God, before I could catch myself this morning,
negative thoughts pulled me under, far from you.
I woke up feeling the shame of being less than;
I looked at my life and saw only lack.
When I am in over my head in negativity,
help me swim back to the solace of your grace,
to climb back up the riverbank of your love.

act

Today, forgive yourself for when you get caught up in negative thoughts about yourself. This too shall pass.

Old Wounds Can Reopen
Carol Ann Morrow

reflect

A stray reminder can lead us to relive a long-ago injury—one received, one given. It is humbling to recall that we acted or reacted in anger, with ugliness—that we even hold a grudging memory today.

pray

When you walked the earth, Friend Jesus,
you reached out in kindness, even to those whose intentions
were to harm your reputation or your very body.
Not me.
I have turned my back, I have spoken poison,
I have spread bad news, at times untrue.
You remember it all
and time means nothing to you.
Reach back, reach forward, reach in, reach out.
Close the wounds.
Lighten the scars.
Erase the darkness.
Your forgiveness eclipses my small efforts.
Bless my enemies.
May they be numbered among the saints.

act

I will try to picture one enemy vividly. I will see that person happy and blessed. Let it be so.

To Self-Forgive, Divine

Christopher Heffron

reflect

We're taught to forgive when we are wronged, to turn the other cheek. Sometimes it's even more difficult to forgive ourselves. May this prayer be our first steps in doing just that.

pray

Dear God,
When I sin, I know you are
eager to forgive.
But sometimes I cannot
be quite so merciful with myself.
Teach me to be graceful with others
but also forgiving of myself when I stumble.
Allow peace to fill my heart,
and let me never forget that I am worth finding
when I stray too far.
Amen.

act

Share this prayer with somebody who's struggling with guilt. Remind them that nothing can turn God away from them.

The Power of Forgiveness

Susan Hines-Brigger

reflect

When we are hurt by someone, it's not easy to let that pain go. Forgiveness seems like too big a step to take. But by letting go of the hurt, we are actually freeing ourselves to heal from the hurt.

pray

Dear God,
give me the strength
to release my hurt and anger,
and have the courage
to travel the path
to forgiveness.
I know it won't be
an easy path,
so I ask you
to walk by my side.
Amen.

act

Offer the gift of forgiveness to someone who has hurt you. If you're not able to do this in person, do so in your heart.

Restoring Relationships

Clifford Hennings, OFM

reflect

When we have been hurt or wronged by someone we love, the lasting effect is a strained relationship. Forgiveness isn't just about letting our grievances go. Forgiveness is the path to restoring the love that binds us to God and to one another.

pray

God, shine your loving mercy upon me now.
Let the flames of your spirit sear away
the callouses of my heart.
Soften my spirit.
Remove what estranges me from you
and my sisters and brothers,
that I may live in peace and bear witness to your compassion.
Amen.

act

When you make this prayer today, offer up to God one grievance you have been holding on to. Pray for the grace to be freed from this burden.

acceptance.

In God's Hands

Colleen M. Arnold, MD

reflect

Sometimes my worry about the people I love manifests itself as a desire to control their choices or influence their behavior. I try to keep them safe in a bubble of my own design.

pray

Dear Lord, it is so hard to relinquish control
over the lives of the people I love.
Please help me remember that only you see the whole picture
and know what's best for them.
Help me trust that you will guide them along the path ahead
far better than I can.
Amen.

act

Picture the face of a loved one for whom you often worry cupped in your hands. Raise your hands to God and imagine him gently taking the face you love into his own strong hands. Then let go.

St. Clare's Jar
Maureen O'Brien

reflect

In your readings, have you already come across the suggestion to find an empty jar? In a time of trouble, St. Clare of Assisi left out an empty jar, which was found full of oil. Today can we not be so afraid of an emptiness in our lives?

pray

Today I choose to behold the beauty of that empty jar.
How it shines and reflects: This clear glass,
a symbol of space inside me, a place for you to find.
I won't rush around trying to force
something other than you to fill it.
Instead I will rejoice in how St. Clare helps me see the truth
of how beautiful it can be: The emptiness in my own hands,
the emptiness of me.

act

Find a jar to remind you that the emptiness is part of the journey and allow it to bring you peace.

Accepting Limitations
Bruce Epperly

reflect

Toward the end of her life, mystic, social activist, and founder
of the Catholic Worker movement, Dorothy Day was sidelined
by physical ailments. No doubt her infirmity challenged her
patience. Dorothy rose above her limitations by discovering that
her vocation was to pray for the world and for justice. We can pray
for patience, not passivity, discovering what we can do within the
limitations of our lives, remembering our limitations are also the
womb of possibility.

pray

God of restlessness and calm,
I pray for peace in my heart and in the world.
I pray for patience with what I cannot change
and passion and protest for what I can.
Let me recognize there are many possibilities to pursue
in the quest to be your companion in healing the world.
Amen.

act

For whom am I called to pray today? Where do I feel most
impatient? How can I use my feelings of impatience as a catalyst
for personal or social change? From my answers to these
questions, let me act forthrightly and wisely.

Trusting Even When Things Go Wrong

Colleen M. Arnold, MD

r e f l e c t

Despite our desperate prayers, sometimes the lost dog isn't found, the cancer isn't cured, the trip of a lifetime is canceled. It takes trust to remember that even when things don't go the way we want, God is not deaf to our needs and petitions.

p r a y

Dear God,
help me trust that you always want the best for me,
even when life feels wrong.
You don't ignore my pleas;
you hold my hands as I pray them.
You don't turn away from my pain;
you suffer through it with me.
You don't promise my life will be easy;
you promise to walk alongside me in it.
Help me remember that on even the worst of days,
you are with me.
Amen.

a c t

Make a list of five ways that God helped you get through a recent event that didn't go as you wanted.

In Order to Love, Let Go
Bruce Epperly

reflect

When we love, others' lives become as important as our own. We balance our self-interest with affirming their deepest needs. We discover that the sacrifices we make are more than compensated by a sense of loving connection, openheartedness, and the recognition that we are bringing joy and beauty to another person and to the world.

pray

Loving God, I thank you for the love I received
and the opportunity to love today.
I thank you for those who sacrificed for my well-being,
and I commit myself to sacrifice for the well-being of others.
Let my focus go from self-interest to care for others:
my community and world loyalty.
Amen.

act

Today I will let my love flow to others in acts of kindness and sacrifice. I will tangibly and concretely love others as I love myself.

The Hands of Our Mother

Maureen O'Brien

r e f l e c t

Even the smallest of misunderstandings can grow into a web of confusion and hurt feelings. Has some issue in your life felt like a knot that only grows tighter? Think of a time you tried to untie a "knot" in your life. Did you get frustrated? Remember how that frustration felt.

p r a y

Mary, of all your lovely names—Cause of Our Joy, Mystical Rose, the Undoer of Knots calls to the tangled-up world right now.
In these truly painful times, it brings comfort to trust
the grace of your hands.
You unravel the knots of cynicism, despair, and hopelessness
with the same soft, holy hands that held
your baby when he was radiant,
surrounded by angels above his manger.
Yes, those same perfect hands will untwist
the tightest of our knots.

a c t

Today, ask the patient and gentle Mary, Undoer of Knots, to place her hands on the sorrows and challenges that you bring to her.

Days in the Desert

Stephen Copeland

reflect

Whether it's waiting or working, it can sometimes feel like we
are journeying through the desert with no end in sight. But it's
often in the desert that we learn the most about God, ourselves,
and what we are grateful for in the present. May this prayer be a
reminder of the spiritual landscape of the desert.

pray

In these days that blur together,
may grace surprise me evermore.
When the world stops turning,
may I still see the splendor of earth.
As I labor beneath the scorching sun,
may I be grateful for the work.
Thank you, Lord, for desert days
that help me love you all the more.

act

Read this simple prayer in the morning, afternoon, and evening.
Take note of how you experienced God's love in the hours before,
or what you are most thankful for in the present moment.

You're Invited to Begin Again

Maureen O'Brien

r e f l e c t

We're troubled, sometimes even haunted, by the past—things we've done, didn't do, or wish we had done differently. Begin today thinking of the words of Mother Teresa, "Do not let the past disturb you, just leave everything in the Sacred Heart and begin again in joy." Perhaps letting go opens an avenue to loving someone that wasn't there before.

p r a y

How beautiful to envision the past within the Sacred Heart,
so I no longer have to carry it. It's heavy!
Instead of sifting through all the life-changing hurts in my mind,
let me let go of it all.
Today I can say yes to the invitation,
as if to a spur-of-the-moment party,
to begin again, to begin again—in joy.

a c t

Imagine putting some part of your past that you feel is still not resolved in the Sacred Heart of Jesus, where you can truly let it go. If you feel just a bit lighter, celebrate it.

patience and peace.

Positive Boundaries

Bond Strong

reflect

Jesus often retreated by himself to pray during his ministry. He was famously caught napping on a boat during a storm. He was a person who valued rest and had clear boundaries, yet he also suffered immensely and willingly on behalf of others. What does his example tell us about the responsibility to steward our lives and time well?

pray

Lord Jesus, you lived a perfectly balanced life.
You revealed to us what a life lived in service to others looks like,
but also what it takes to live a life in service of others.
It takes intentionality and rest to be able to do what we must.
Grant us the grace to discern when we need to rest
and when we need to act.
Amen.

act

Are you failing to take the time to rest so you are able to serve? If so, take time this week to recharge.

Creating Space

Julia Walsh, FSPA

reflect

The God who made the expanding universe also created your beautiful body. In each mystery, there is open space. Consider the sacred spaces in your life: your tables, your home, your church, your heart. Are your spaces open to receive whoever God sends?

pray

God of the universe, every space you have created is sacred,
no matter how enormous or tiny.
Thank you for the sacred spaces I am able to share.
Help me to be like you, open and inclusive to others,
so all may come to know the sacredness of who they are.
Amen.

act

Create a sacred space in your home and consider how you can invite others to join you for prayer or sharing on that holy ground.

Growing in Patience

Shannon K. Evans

reflect

Patience is not simply a trait that one either does or does not possess; patience is a virtue that one chooses to develop. In light of this choice, may this prayer assist you in your inner growth.

pray

Loving God,
your patience with me
is so tender and merciful;
yet I struggle
to extend that patience
to my loved ones, coworkers, neighbors,
and even to myself.
As I pray to grow more patient,
I know that it is also a choice
to be repeatedly made.
I need your grace
to choose to live a slow and steady
life of love.
Amen.

act

Light a candle and leave it in a place where you will see it often today. Let the lit candle remind you of your intention to choose patience each time you pass.

A Lasting Peace

Christopher Heffron

reflect

We may not be able to control what goes on in the world, but we can control how we react to it. This prayer can help us stay focused.

pray

Dear God,
When life is noisy, I seek quiet.
When my heart is restless,
I crave stillness.
For in that soundless space,
I know that joy awaits me.
Wrap my soul in light
and grace me
with the hope I need
to carry on.
In your arms I find the peace
my soul desires.
Amen.

act

Life can be noisy, but it shouldn't disturb our peace of mind. Close your eyes, breathe deeply, and spend a moment of quiet prayer with God. Repeat.

Time to Slow Down
Susan Hines-Brigger

reflect
___

We live in a fast-paced society. Because of that, we have become accustomed to not waiting for things. By doing so, we often miss what we can learn and experience when we have patience and wait for things to unfold just as they should.

pray
___

Dear God,
remind us
that all things will happen
in the appropriate time.
It is through waiting
that we are able
to experience so many
of life's blessings.
Things such as flowers,
babies, seasons,
and more all come
after a period
of patient waiting.
Help us to find joy
and embrace that time.
Amen.

act
___

The next time you're starting to lose your patience stop, close your eyes, and count to ten—or take a deep breath.

Holy Humdrum
Maureen O'Brien

reflect

Do you ever feel swept away with the tide of daily life? Think of the words of Psalm 139:3, "You sift through my travels and my rest; with all my ways you are familiar."

pray

God, you are there in struggle,
and so I can let go of my anger and frustration
that I'm doing soulless tasks alone, without support.
Paying bills.
Medical appointments.
Being put on hold, again.
All the disconnections can feel so empty.
But you are there, ever holy!
In those moments my life feels drained of all that is sacred,
but *all* of it is sacred with you there.
While filling the gas tank, I notice the clouds in blue sky.
How wispy they are, traveling the same direction as me.

act

Instead of fighting the mundane and boring today, flip it and see if you can find something sacred in the act—a deeper connection lurking underneath. If you discover something unexpected in the process, journal about it to nurture this type of thinking.

Breathing Exercises
Natalie Ryan

reflect

So often we try to control every part of our lives, living by planners, organization, and what's next. We go through the week feeling winded and exhausted. It's time to stop, to pause, to breathe.

pray

God, I am rushing from thing to thing.
I am trying to accomplish all that I can.
I forget that you are with me.
With you all things are possible.
If only I believe.
With you the yoke is easy and burden light.
Remind me, Lord, to trust so that I may find
peace and joy in my daily walk with you.
Amen.

act

Take five to ten minutes today to do a breathing exercise. Breathe in through the nose slowly for seven seconds, and exhale slowly through the mouth for eight seconds. Repeat this, paying attention to the rise and fall of the belly. Breathe in God's love and breathe out God's life.

Coffee and Mindfulness
Bond Strong

reflect

We often go about our day without thought: we slurp our cup of coffee or tea while driving or inhale a burger on the go. Our food is a lost opportunity for connection—with ourselves, those around us, and the divine.

pray

God who made our bodies to function so well, created the plants and animals we eat, and guided those who prepare our food or gather round our table, thank you for the sustenance, the energy, and the opportunity to slow down and acknowledge your presence.
When we allow life to move too quickly—even though it's almost always an unconscious decision—we are missing out on the sacredness of the present.
In the hurried moments, may we remember to take a deep breath, and call to mind that you are in our presence—yes, even in line at the grocery, as we eat lunch while working, as we recite a prayer from rote memory.
May this conscious interruption enhance our spirits.
Amen.

act

If you go through a drive-thru or to a coffee shop this week, take a moment to make eye contact with the server. Commit one morning to sipping an entire cup of coffee or tea in a chair in silence without any distractions.

Paths Cleared

Natalie Ryan

reflect

God has parted seas. He has shut the mouths of lions. He has moved mountains. He has shielded from flames and storms. God enlivens dry bones and converts graves to gardens. Only God can do these things. Why do I doubt?

pray

Lord, help me to trust this process—to trust you.
I cannot see in the storm, but your mighty power protects me, your mercy mends me.
Convert my doubt to devotion—
praying confidently for your love for me.
Amen.

act

Print off a labyrinth and trace it slowly with your finger. Start from the outside and move inside. Then move inside to outside. Repeat this process as you pray.

This Is My Body
Carol Ann Morrow

reflect

When St. Francis was dying, he apologized to Brother Body for the harsh treatment he issued so often. I often feel critical of my own body, seldom because of penances, but because of excess or unreasonable expectations.

pray

Lord God,
you have allowed me to become a tabernacle.
When I receive you in our recurring Last Supper,
I become the scriptural Ark of the Covenant.
My daily self is blessed, as the work of your hands.
Yet I fail to respect the glory of my muscles,
bones and ligaments.
I want to dance, but I stumble.
I don't thank you enough for the miracle
of all my senses.
I apologize.
Straighten my back today.
Walk with me.
May this inner beauty be manifest.

act

I will work through my body to honor you today. I will use my strengths as you inspire me.

courage.

Jesus, Help My Unbelief!
Patricia Breen

reflect

The incident of Thomas doubting Jesus in a post-Resurrection sighting reminds us that Jesus always comes and meets us right where we are, even when his presence brings uncomfortable feelings or emotions.

pray

Dear Jesus,
I do believe in you—please heal my unbelief.
When life gets hard or messy,
help me to trust the promises
you have spoken over my life and destiny.
Help me believe even when I cannot see the road ahead.
Amen.

act

Spend some time praying with the story of Thomas' doubting, found in John 20:19-31. Put yourself in the scene and ask Jesus what he wishes to say to you.

Remember the Nation

Stephen Copeland

r e f l e c t

There are real problems in our beloved country, but we are
here—in this place, in this moment—and are therefore called to be
stewards of what we've received, in whatever state we received
it. May we do the hard work to invest ourselves in a hope and
liberty that unites us rather than doing the easy thing and caving
to fear, hopelessness, or hate.

p r a y

Today I pray for the land I love:
once a beacon for the broken once a symbol of salvation,
before the bully had a bullhorn, before we lost our reputation,
before revolution replaced reform, before pundits preyed on fear,
cherry-picking information; back when apathy was a luxury,
when leadership was expected, when open discourse was the
norm—can our soul be resurrected?
Guide me, Lord, to love and serve, to steward what you gave,
to refuse to cave to hopelessness and clean up this mess
we made.

a c t

When you become discouraged today by the state of our nation,
allow that grief to exist and name your concerns. Get specific.
But also surrender your frustration to God and ask yourself: How
can I be a steward today of what I've received?

Fear Has Said Its Prayers

Bruce Epperly

reflect

It has been said that courage is fear that has said its prayers.
When we pray our fears, we discover that we are not alone. We
discover that God is with us and that nothing can separate us
from the love of God. We can act courageously—despite our
fears—to make the world a better place.

pray

Loving God,
I place my fear in your hands.
You know my strengths
just as you know my weakness.
Let me trust that when I go through the darkest valley
you are with me, surrounding me, empowering me,
guiding and strengthening me
so I can respond with courage
to bring justice, reconciliation, and love
to the world around me.
Amen.

act

What situation needs your attention, despite your fears? Place
your fears in God's hands and ask God to give you courage. Then,
with God's guidance, respond wisely and bravely to difficult
situations.

Come Alive, Dry Bones!

Vanesa Zuleta Goldberg

reflect

When God tells the prophet Ezekiel to prophesy and command dry bones to come back to life, it's a compelling image. The same voice that once commanded Ezekiel compels our own bones to rise out of our shame into the light of God.

pray

God of life,
who brought back dry bones in a desert valley,
speak to my bones today,
to my flesh, to my heart.
May I know of life—life to the fullest—by simply listening
to your voice today.
God of Ezekiel, may you prophesy over my dry bones
and bring me into your light.
Amen.

act

Reflect today on where God is calling you to come fully alive in your life.

Everyday Courage

Shannon K. Evans

reflect

When we think about having courage, we usually imagine extraordinary circumstances and heroic acts of bravery. But for most of us, living courageously is a matter of choosing it with quiet resolution day after day.

pray

God who sustains me,
life is difficult and my trials afflict me.
No one understands how hard it can be
to just press on.
Restore my heart and my hope,
O God, fill me with the courage it takes
to get out of bed in the morning
and do my best all over again.
Help me feel your pride in me,
and may your delight give me strength.
Amen.

act

Take this moment to reflect on your life circumstances—especially the area that is currently requiring courage of you. Sit in silence for a moment and let the Holy Spirit fill you with the knowledge that your courage is seen and honored.

Loving the Big Bad Wolf
Bruce Epperly

reflect

Hearing that a wolf was terrorizing the town of Gubbio, Francis
of Assisi reached out to the wolf, befriending it and reconciling
it with the townsfolk, who agreed to feed the animal. Even the
most difficult of people need our love. While we may not be as
successful in taming the wild beasts in others as Francis was, we
can still see them as God's beloved children with the same basic
needs as ourselves.

pray

God of power and love, help me see your presence
in the wild beasts that trouble me.
Give me courage to reach out, and love to respond.
Help me share your love in ways that bring healing
and promote justice
and to bring your realm to earth as it is in heaven.
Amen.

act

As you listen to the news, remind yourself to see the holiness in
those you are tempted to fear or hate. Pray for those from whom
you feel alienated and seek justice for those who may be harmed
by the behaviors of others.

Have a Courageous Heart

Clifford Hennings, OFM

reflect

The difference between courage and brashness is wisdom. The
fool may go into challenges with gusto but will fail. Courage
does not mean a lack of fear. Courage is moving forward despite
fear. Christian courage means trusting that the Lord is with you
even in times of trouble. Is there something you've been putting
off doing because it makes you anxious just thinking about it?
Ignoring these things doesn't make them go away. They only get
more frightful for us.

pray

God of might, be my surety as I face the difficulties that lie ahead.
Steady my hand that I may do the work you have set before me.
Remove the obstacles that keep me from moving forward
and lead the way that I may follow.
Amen.

act

Ask God for the grace to take your first step today in doing what
you know must be done.

Decision at Daybreak

Maureen O'Brien

reflect

No matter how much we practice patience, no matter how much we pray, sometimes the morning arrives when we must take the action we've been contemplating, and it can be scary. No matter our choices, God will give us the courage to act.

pray

Dear God, you know I've taken this decision slowly.

I've prayed at Mass and at midnight.

I've sought advice, tried to do it right.

I've been holding on. And now that time is here.

Yes, today is the day.

Give me the courage I need to surrender to your will.

I long to let go!

The birds in your sky make it look so easy to glide and trust.

Help me do what I know I must do.

If only it were that simple, to just go where your winds blow.

act

If you face a hard decision today, know that you've tried your best to pray to make the right choice. Let yourself lie down and rest. Honor how hard it's been.

Called to Be Vulnerable

Herman Sutter

reflect

When we feel vulnerable we often become anxious and frightened. But it is through our vulnerability that God blesses the world. Think of Abraham, called to leave the security of his home and go to an unknown land; it was there that he would become a blessing.

pray

Dear Lord, take me out of my comfort zone today
and make me a blessing to all who meet me this day.
Remind me that we are on this journey of life together.
May my fear of opening up to those around me
be overcome by the promise and potential
of the human connection.

act

Speak to someone you don't know well. Or call someone you haven't spoken to in a long time. And really listen. It may feel awkward at first, but that is part of being vulnerable, of becoming a blessing.

His Lantern

Maureen O'Brien

reflect

If we wake with troubled or lonely hearts, we can remember right away that we are not alone; we can close our eyes and begin our day by envisioning the comfort of God's light. No matter our situation, he promises to find us.

pray

God, I awake with anxiety.
My feelings are tossed
like the surface of a bottomless sea.
Guide me to trust
that you are here.
Help me see the tiny speck of hope
on the bleak horizon.
There it is, your lantern—
yellow rays of light
spilling across the waves.
Your love, headed my way.
Growing brighter and nearer.
Forever finding me.

act

There are so many lights in our lives, dispelling the dark. See if you can find them today: the lamps, the streetlights, the headlights, the stars. Look at how the sun moves east to west. Really look at how the darkness disappears.

compassion.

The People in My Path

Colleen M. Arnold, MD

reflect

Sometimes we are so busy and distracted we don't even notice
the people God places in our paths. We miss out on the chance to
be his hands and feet in the world.

pray

Dear God, I am sorry that my busyness
keeps me from noticing your people—
the coworker having a bad day,
the friend who needs a listening ear,
the neighbor going to bed hungry.
I'm sorry I miss these opportunities to show your love to others.
Please help me slow down and pay attention.
Open my eyes to see others as you do.
Then, open my heart to love them as you do.
Amen.

act

Make eye contact with the people you encounter today and give
them your full attention. You don't have to have all the answers
to their problems; your presence and consideration will be most
welcome.

Meet People Where They Are

Patricia Breen

reflect

The encounter of Jesus meeting the Samaritan woman (John 4:4-26) right where she was in her life led to her own profound conversion, which led her to go and tell the whole town about what had happened.

pray

Jesus, you met the Samaritan woman
right where she was,
even if her life was a mess.
May this sacred encounter be a powerful reminder
to all of us as we strive to meet others
with pastoral care and compassion.
Amen.

act

Who in your life do you need to meet right where they are? Ask Jesus to reveal that person to you, and then love them right where they are.

Setting an Intention

Bruce Epperly

reflect

Stephen Covey, author of *Seven Habits of Highly Effective People*, counseled that we should begin with the end in mind. We should consider what we really want to happen in every situation. We should consider how we might contribute to the well-being of others and ourselves and act accordingly. Let us act with intentionality to bring peace on earth and good will to all.

Pray

Loving God, help me keep my eyes fixed on your goals.
Let me act with awareness,
prayerfully seeking to do your will in every situation.
Help me be faithful to my calling as your beloved child
and companion in healing the world.
Amen.

Act

In every situation ask: "What would Jesus want me to do? How might I share God's light and love, and bring out the best in others? How might I live out my vocation as God's healing companion?"

Tear Down the Walls of Indifference
Bruce Epperly

reflect

The pain of the world challenges us to go from apathy to empathy, from avoidance of pain to recognizing and responding to the pain and joy around you. The way of Jesus challenges us to embrace the pain and joy of the world and respond courageously and lovingly as God's healing companions to those who suffer.

pray

God of all creation,
Open my heart
to the pain and joy of the world.
Open my senses
to the sounds of happiness and sorrow.
Break down the barriers of apathy
that I might have large-spirited empathy.
Let me strive to bring joy to all creation
and all your beloved children.
Amen.

act

Let me pause to notice the pain of the world, suffering of individuals, and injustice in my country. I will intentionally open to the struggles of others, and prayerfully consider how I can be most helpful to them. Let me feel kinship with the least of these and respond with respect and compassion.

For All First Responders

Clifford Hennings, OFM

reflect
___

We often take for granted there is someone to help us in our time
of need. When things are going well, they go unnoticed. Only
when we need them do we think of them. Let us pray for those
people now.

pray
___

Christ,
you chose to become
a servant to all,
taking on the weight of our sin,
braving ridicule, pain, and death,
so you might rescue us
and bring us to life again.
Be with those who face danger
for the sake of others,
guide and protect them this day,
and give me a heart full of gratitude for them.
Amen.

act
___

Today, offer a simple gesture of gratitude to a first responder and
let them know you have prayed for them.

Our Weary Healthcare Workers
Shannon K. Evans

reflect

The COVID-19 pandemic made us more aware than ever of the
trauma endured by healthcare workers around the world. Let us
not forget their sacrifice and ongoing commitment to care for
others.

pray

Oh Great Physician, you know the weariness
of healthcare workers right now.
Our doctors, nurses, clinic and hospital staff
feel as though they are fraying at the seams
with nothing left to give.
You grieved with them, consoled them, and held them
through the endless months of the pandemic.
Continue to let your presence be with them.
You have brought them to our minds,
prompted us to pray for them,
reminded us to speak blessing over them.
Continue to press them on our hearts.
And may we, as their loved ones, make choices
that will protect them—mind, body, and soul.
Amen.

act

Write a thank-you card to at least one healthcare worker you
know for the way they have served their communities during
the pandemic.

For Those Who Are Alone

Clifford Hennings, OFM

reflect

The elderly and infirm are particularly vulnerable to the effects of loneliness and neglect. Let us pray now for all who find themselves alone.

pray

Lord,
you are the Good Shepherd.
When one of your flock
is lost,
you seek them out
and bring them back
into your embrace.
Be with those
who are lonely
and have no one
to care for them.
Let them know your presence
and the care of people
of good will.
Amen.

act

If you know someone who lives alone, consider giving that person a call today. Ask how they are doing and let them know you are offering this prayer for them today.

Actively Caring for Others
Susan Hines-Brigger

reflect

A popular quote from TV's Mister Rogers reminds us that in times of tragedy and chaos, we should "look for the helpers." Seeing people reaching out in compassion calms our fears and reminds us that we're not alone in our need. At some point in our lives, we will all need help. We will likely also be called upon to offer help to others.

pray

Dear God,
give me the strength
to reach out for help
when I need it most.
Remind me that there is no weakness
in seeking help.
Likewise, lead me to places
where I can assist others
in their times of need.
May we all remember
to reach out and lift each other up
for the glory of God.
Amen.

act

Seek out an act of service today. It doesn't have to be big. Acts of service can be as simple as calling and checking on your parents, helping your child with homework, or being a listening ear for a friend.

The Forgotten Commandment

Richard Patterson

reflect

We all know we are called to love our neighbor, but many of us forget the rest of that commandment—to love ourselves. Some confuse love of self with being self-centered. Others can't get past guilt or regret. Jesus is there to help us learn. Jesus can help us quiet the inner voice of condemnation and replace it with his gentle words, "I am with you always."

pray

Lord, teach me to love myself.
Guide me to see myself through your eyes.
I try to reach out to my neighbor with loving compassion.
Help me to do the same for myself.
May I speak words of kindness to myself
and quiet the inner voice of judgment.

act

At the end of each day, write down something you did well that day. It can be something as simple as, "I cooked a good meal" or "I enjoyed playing with my child."

Look Beyond the Mirror

Susan Hines-Brigger

reflect

Sometimes when we look in the mirror, we say things to ourselves that we would never say to someone else. We find all our flaws, all the things we wish were different. But in doing so, we forget that we are wonderfully made in God's image. We also forget that there is a great deal underneath what we see in the mirror. What's inside matters, too. Sometimes we just have to look deeper.

pray

Lord, help us to remember that
when we look at ourselves,
we are also gazing at your face.
May we remember
that we are so much more than
what we see on the outside.
And may we celebrate ourselves as children of God.

act

Write down five things that you love about yourself—both inside and out.

social justice.

Let Justice Flow Like a River

Vanesa Zuleta Goldberg

reflect

Dorothy Day was a social activist, pacifist, advocate for the underprivileged, and journalist. She lived in a time replete with injustice against others, and she actively refused to fade into all the noise. Rather, Dorothy used her voice to make space for the marginalized, and encountered Christ in those who lived at the margins. Her life—marked by works of justice and commitment to solidarity—serves as a reminder of the gospel message.

pray

God at the margins, you who know the names and faces
of the poor, the oppressed, the marginalized.
May we encounter you at the margins.
May we resist the temptation of power
that comes at the cost of the other.
And may we come to encounter your heart
in our marginalized brothers and sisters.
Let there come forth from your heart and our hearts rivers of
justice that give us all everlasting life.
Amen.

act

Today, spend some time learning about Dorothy Day's legacy, the Catholic Worker Movement. Let it inspire you to donate your time, money, or prayer to promoting the mission of peacemaking that marked Dorothy's life.

Justice Requires Openness

Shannon K. Evans

reflect

To follow Jesus is to commit ourselves to justice. This requires inward change more often than we would like and can be a complicated journey. May this prayer help us live the way of Jesus more authentically in our own hearts.

pray

Jesus,
I sometimes resist when my perspective
is challenged, when others cry "injustice"
over something I cannot see.
Make my heart humble and teachable
to witness the experience of others
so that I can best discern where the pursuit
of justice leads.
Amen.

act

Identify one thing that has been labeled a "justice issue" but makes you feel uncomfortable. Find at least one thoughtful, clear-headed voice who can share an opposing perspective with you. Resolve to read or listen to that person's words with an open mind.

The Last Will Be First

Christopher Heffron

reflect

When I once asked a friar if I should give money to homeless
people, knowing that they may spend it on something
destructive, he said, "Of course! Would you rather err on the side
of charity or suspicion?" I've never forgotten those words—and
they are the heartbeat of this prayer.

pray

Dear God,
too often I take
for granted my blessings:
home, health, family, security.
But not everyone
is so fortunate.
Let me give what I can
to those in need.
Let me look into the eyes
of those from whom we often turn away.
Because they are, as I am,
your child: loved and favored.
Amen.

act

Offer this prayer in solidarity with those who struggle on the
periphery. They are no less cherished by God than you or I.

We're Called to Make 'Good Trouble'

Patricia Breen

reflect

The late congressman John Lewis was known for his lifetime work fighting racism through his words calling people to make, "good trouble, necessary trouble." A freedom fighter deeply inspired by the work of Dr. Martin Luther King Jr., Lewis tirelessly poured out his life for racial justice and healing in our nation until the day he died.

pray

Spirit of Truth, there is power when an individual stands up for the truth of their convictions.
You inspired Congressman John Lewis to work and advocate for the way of peace—the way of love and nonviolence.
Through his witness, may we be inspired to listen to where the Spirit living in us calls us to move.
Amen.

act

Ask the Holy Spirit, "Where am I called to make good trouble today for the Kingdom of God?"

A Place at the Table
Vanesa Zuleta Goldberg

r e f l e c t

Sometimes it feels like we don't have a place at the table. Yet the promise of our faith is that Jesus welcomes us all to the table as we rejoice in his love for us. Reflect today on the friendship that Christ had with his disciples.

p r a y

Welcoming Christ, you who have created this table
with your carpenter hands,
who sat at it with your friends countless years ago,
remind me that I, too, can sit at this table—
that I, too, am worthy to sit here and know of your love for me.
Today, dispel from me any lie that tells me
this table does not want me here.
Welcoming Christ, beckon me to the table.
Amen.

a c t

Journey with the narratives in the Gospels and let them be a reminder that Christ calls you into the same friendship he shared with the disciples, to sit with him at the table.

Sealed with a Prayer
Carol Ann Morrow

r e f l e c t

Each time I exercise my right to vote, I wonder whether I chose well. I hear and read of many disagreements and struggles, even inability to come to good decisions for the country.

p r a y

Creator of Eden, we no longer dwell there with you.

We quarrel over laws, ordinances, even petty customs.

Return us to a land of harmony.

Bless us as we try to be good citizens.

Help us respect the rights of all our neighbors.

a c t

I will send an email or post a message affirming one of my elected officials. I will seal it with a prayer.

An Inspiration against Racism

Patricia Breen

reflect

Over the course of her life, St. Katharine Drexel focused her
energy on the material and spiritual well-being of African
Americans and Native Americans. Mother Katharine's dedicated
efforts can inspire us and be a model for us as we work to uproot
systemic racist ideas in our Church and in the world.

pray

Dear Jesus, you inspired and emboldened
Katharine Drexel to work for justice
for underserved groups of people.
Her life left a lasting legacy.
She is a model to all Christians
fighting against racist principles and ideas
alive in the world, our hearts, and the Church.
We ask St. Katharine's intercession
for us in this important work.
Amen.

act

Choose one or two resources—books, movies, TV shows—to
better educate yourself on how to fight the evils of racism right
where God has placed you.

Housing for All

Shannon K. Evans

reflect

Basic human dignity should entitle each of us to have shelter from the elements and a place on earth to call our own. Housing should be a simple human right, and yet many people around the world do not have a home to which to return. The least we can do is remember them and pray for justice for them in the future.

pray

Dear God, your Scriptures tell us
we can hide in the shelter of your wings.
Today, I pray for such comfort for my fellow human beings
who are without the safety of a home.
Protect them.
Watch over them.
Keep them safe from harm and despair.
I pray for policy changes that might make the future
a more just one for all people.
I pray for a future where every
human being has a place to call home.
Until that day comes,
show me what more I can do to hasten it,
and fill me with compassion for those who still wait.
Amen.

act

Contact the nearest temporary housing shelter and ask what they need that you might be able to donate.

For Those Who Work the Land

Clifford Hennings, OFM

reflect

In the developed world, many take the availability of food for granted. We go to the store and are presented with countless choices. Yet behind all that food is the sweat from someone's hard labor. Let us pray for them today.

pray

Almighty and loving Father,
be with those who till the earth.
Guide their hands
and bless their harvest,
that they may reap
the rewards of their labor,
and all may share in their bounty.
Amen.

act

If you're going grocery shopping today, when you get your produce, offer this prayer for the farmers who worked the soil. If you aren't, offer this prayer before your meals.

Brothers and Sisters in Christ

Daniel Imwalle

reflect

The sad history of injustices committed against Asians in America has long been overlooked. Now is the time to reckon with our past as we look to a brighter future in our nation for all.

pray

Lord, help us do the hard work of looking within
—as individuals and as a society—
and uprooting the ugliness of racism.
In its place, may we instead foster love and respect
among all peoples.
In particular today, we offer up a prayer
for the protection of those of Asian descent,
as they struggle against the evils of racism.
May you reveal to those of us from other racial and
ethnic groups the beauty of the varied Asian cultures,
traditions, cuisines, and arts.
May we be continually reminded of the inherent value of
our Asian brothers and sisters,
and may we remember those who have lost their lives
because of violence fueled by racism.
Amen.

act

Challenge racism in your daily life through conversations with friends or family members who may harbor resentments toward a particular group of people.

Let Justice Come Alive Today

Bruce Epperly

reflect

We can't wait for justice in our world. We can't put off the quest for equality. We must embody justice today, plan for justice today, and be the justice we want to see in the world. In committing ourselves to contemplative activism, let us take time to pray and then join our prayers with protest.

pray

God of tomorrow's dreams,
let there be peace on earth
and let it begin with me.
Let there be justice today
and let me be its prophet.
Let me feel the pain of the world
and respond with compassion.
Let me be just in every dealing
and out of my quest for integrity
let me embody your realm of shalom.
Amen.

act

Where do you see racism and injustice? What persons are forgotten and marginalized? Whose voices are silenced or forgotten in your community and the nation? Ask God for guidance for your justice-seeking, and when you receive an answer, make a commitment to respond with compassion and challenge.

About the Authors

Colleen M. Arnold, MD, a physician and writer residing in Lexington, Virginia, also holds a master's degree in pastoral ministry. Her website is ColleenArnold.org.

Patricia Breen lives and works in the Detroit area. She holds a master's degree in pastoral studies from Sacred Heart Major Seminary and is the ministry formation manager for Ascension, a faith-based health-care organization.

Stephen Copeland is an Indiana native who now lives in Charlotte, North Carolina, with his wife and son, Indy. His new memoir, *In the House of Rising Sounds*, is based around an historic blues venue and is an exploration of what the ancient Celts describe as "thin spaces." He has been published widely in *St. Anthony Messenger* magazine and other resources offered by Franciscan Media.

Theresa Doyle-Nelson enjoys researching and writing about holy people from the Bible and is the author of *Saints in Scripture*. She and her husband, Chad, make their home in the Texas Hill Country and have three children and seven grandchildren. You can find more of Theresa's writing online at TheresaDoyle-Nelson.blogspot.com.

Rev. Dr. Bruce G. Epperly has served as a congregational pastor, university chaplain, professor, and seminary administrator for over forty years. He is the author of more than 50 books on practical theology, ministry, and spirituality, healing and wholeness, and process theology. He lives on Cape Cod, Massachusetts, with his wife, Rev. Dr. Katherine Gould Epperly, his son, daughter-in-law, and grandchildren.

Shannon K. Evans is the author of *Embracing Weakness, Rewilding Motherhood,* and *Luminous: A 30-Day Journal for Accepting Your Body, Honoring Your Soul, and Finding Your Joy.* She and her family make their home in central Iowa.

Vanesa Zuleta Goldberg has worked in youth ministry for many years. She received her bachelor's in theology at Providence College and her master's in theology and ministry from Boston College School of Theology and Ministry. Her work is centered on the pastoral praxis of creating spaces for ongoing liberation for young people from all walks of life.

Christopher Heffron is the editorial director at Franciscan Media. This writer/editor loves urban hiking, pop culture, and useless information.

Clifford Hennings, OFM, is the associate pastor of the Church of the Holy Family in Novi, Michigan. He received a bachelor's degree in Catholic studies from DePaul University and a Master of Divinity from Catholic Theological Union. He contributes regularly to Franciscan Media and *St. Anthony Messenger.*

Susan Hines-Brigger is an executive editor of *St. Anthony Messenger* magazine. She has worked at Franciscan Media for over twenty-eight years. She and her husband, Mark, are the parents of four children.

Daniel Imwalle serves as the managing editor of St. *Anthony Messenger*. He also contributes to Franciscan Media's popular daily prayer resource, *Pause+Pray*. When he isn't busy catching stray commas, Daniel is probably writing and playing music. He and his wife, Belinda, make their home in Cincinnati, Ohio.

Carol Ann Morrow is a former editor at *St. Anthony Messenger* and the author of *A Retreat with Saint Anthony: Finding Our Way* (Franciscan Media). She lives in Northern Kentucky.

Maureen O'Brien's award-winning short stories and poems have been published widely in magazines and anthologies. She lives in Connecticut, where she taught creative writing to teenagers for twenty-five years. She holds an MA in creative writing and a BA in philosophy and religion. Her latest book is *Gather the Fragments: My Year of Finding God's Love* (Franciscan Media).

Richard B. Patterson, PhD, is a clinical psychologist who practices in El Paso, Texas. Over the years he has contributed several articles to *St. Anthony Messenger*.

Natalie Ryan is an Indianapolis native who has moved to Northern Kentucky. She does parish ministry, is a writer and an artist, and is also a spiritual director. She loves to see how God is working in others' lives, which helps her find him more clearly in her own life.

Bond Strong lives in the mountains of southwest Virginia with her husband, Reece, and two sons, Willis and Harmon. Along with contributing to *Pause+Pray*, *Bond* has also written for several online platforms including *FemCatholic* and *Blessed Is She*.

Herman Sutter is a school librarian, author, and poet who resides in Houston, Texas. To read more of his work, visit WorldBeforeGrace.blogspot.com.

Sister Julia Walsh is a Franciscan Sister of Perpetual Adoration who is part of the Fireplace Community in Chicago. She serves as a spiritual director and vocation minister. Her writing can be found in *America, Global Sisters Report, St. Anthony Messenger,* and elsewhere. Find her podcast and blog at MessyJesusBusiness.com.